The Trail of Tears

Explore the Takeover of Nations from Beginning to End

Adrian Ramos, **History** Compacted

ISBN: 9781671420687

Table of Contents

A Note

From History Compacted

Hi there!

This is Jason Chen, founder of History Compacted. Before you continue your journey to the past, I want to take a quick moment to explain our position on history and the purpose of our books.

To us, history is more than just facts, dates, and names. We see history as pieces of stories that led to the world we know today. Besides, it makes it much more fun seeing it that way too.

That is why History Compacted was created: to tell amazing stories of the past and hopefully inspire you to search for more. After all, history would be too big for any one book. But what each book can give you is a piece of the puzzle to help you get to that fuller picture.

Lastly, I want to acknowledge the fact that history is often told from different perspectives. Depending on the topic and your upbringing, you might agree or disagree with how we present the facts. I understand disagreements are inevitable. That is why with a team of diverse writers, we aim to tell each story from a more neutral perspective. I hope this note can help you better understand our position and goals.

Now without further ado, let your journey to the past begin!

Introduction

"...Many fell by the wayside, too faint with hunger or too weak to keep up with the rest. The aged, feeble, and sick were left to perish by the wayside. A crude bed was quickly prepared for these sick and weary people. Only a bowl of water was left within reach, thus they were left to suffer and die alone. The little children piteously cried day after day from weariness, hunger, and illness. Many of the men, women, and even the children were forced to walk. They were once happy children— left without mother and father—crying could not bring consolation to those children."—Sallie Farney, a Creek woman

This bleak excerpt comes to us from a much longer story of exile and sorrow. It is an eyewitness account from a woman of the Creek tribe, put in writing by way of her granddaughter, Mary Hill.

The story was repeated verbatim because Sallie Farney had told it many times before her death. Mary retold this story in a 1937 interview with a field worker who was collecting Native American family histories to compile into the *Indian-Pioneer History Collection.*

Before this historical collection was made, accounts from Native Americans about what they had suffered were hard to come by. It was easy enough to find the journals of missionaries, U.S. Army officers, or doctors describing the Native American plight from an outside perspective— sometimes sympathetically, sometimes coldly and objectively. But it was next to impossible to read what the Natives saw and thought.

And even with collections like this and others, countless voices remain silenced by the passage of time. We can read, study, and guess what happened to these people, but we can *rarely* feel it.

The hardship Sallie's people endured above was a tragedy shared by countless Creek, Cherokee, Choctaw, and other Native American tribes. What Sallie and her people suffered was a forced migration on a scale never before seen in the history of North America.

Tens of thousands of Native Americans living in the American Southeast were forced out of their ancestral homelands in waves starting in 1830. They came from many different territories, including Georgia, Alabama, or Florida, but they were all bound for the so-called "Indian Territory" reserved for them, west of the Mississippi River.

(Source: https://www.ncdcr.gov/blog/2015/12/29/the-treaty-of-new-echota-and-the-trail-of-tears)

The land was reserved for them by the United States government, which was overseeing the expulsion of their entire societies so that the land they lived on could be freed up and settled by Euro-Americans. It was the culmination of decades of bitter legal battles, and centuries of strained or hostile relations between the colonizer and the colonized.

It has been called many names past and present: a population transfer, an ethnic cleansing, a death march, attempted genocide. But to the people who endured it firsthand, it was known as a "trail of tears and death."

That last description is as awfully true as it is poetic: between thirteen and sixteen thousand people died of exposure, disease, starvation, and violence during the migrations. Families were torn apart, and entire ways of life were completely upended. Worlds that had existed for hundreds of years came to an end in less than twenty.

Contrary to the name, the Trail of Tears was no single trail, but a series of routes over land and sea that led Native Americans away from their ancestral homelands and toward strange new territory west of the Mississippi River. Thousands of miles of deadly wilderness snaked through the American South, to be studied and mapped out by the same brave, unlucky people forced to walk them.

And while the scale of these events was unprecedented, their contents were not. These misdeeds had been done for centuries before, and they would be done for centuries more. Greed and prejudice would continue to plague the first peoples of America up to the present day.

This Trail of Tears is cemented in infamy in the history of the United States of America, and its effects can be felt reverberating through time like the echoing cries of those who perished, endured, or fought against it.

Chapter One

Accommodations & Strife: 1607-1829

It is impossible to condense the entire history of Native American interactions with Anglo-American settlers into a single book, let alone a single chapter. But it is vital to know the context of the Trail of Tears in order to understand why and how it happened, so the attempt will be made anyway.

The Spanish and Portuguese had been actively colonizing the Americas since the end of the fifteenth century. They were later joined by Dutch, British, French, and even Russian or Swedish settlers in the following centuries. Every colonial power left its mark, but this buildup of events focuses mainly on British and later American relationships with Native Americans.

Anglo-Native relations began with the founding of small, unsuccessful settlements or trading posts at around the turn of the seventeenth century. The mysterious case of Roanoke in 1586 was among them, as was the 1602 fort at Cuttyhunk Island. These settlements were soon after abandoned, which makes the establishment of Jamestown, Virginia, in 1607, the starting point for permanent, uninterrupted English settlement of North America.

Algonquian-speaking tribes were the first indigenous groups to meet English settlers. Early contact between the tribes and settlers was tinged with uncertainty, but often cordial and friendly. Local tribes often taught the settlers some of their expertise in order to survive in such unfamiliar territory.

The Powhatan of modern Virginia would give the people of Jamestown food in exchange for trade goods such as metal tools and weapons. The Wampanoag of Massachusetts helped the Pilgrims of Plymouth survive their first winters in America, and in doing so, helped create—or at least mythologize—one of the first Thanksgivings in American history.

But relations could turn cold or even violent just as quickly. By 1609, the governor of Jamestown was ordering raiding parties to threaten the Powhatan and demand more food from them in order to fuel their expanding tobacco industry. Tobacco farming, in turn, led the settlers to convert more and more Powhatan land into plantations.

These intrusions soon sparked the Anglo-Powhatan Wars and the infamous Jamestown Massacre of 1622, which saw about a quarter of the colony's population killed in a surprise attack. These events left a permanent stain on Anglo-Native relations, causing future colonists to fear any and all Native American groups as potential enemies. Treaties between natives and colonists often lasted only while they served the colony's interest. Within the decade, Powhatan lands were almost entirely seized, and the tribe was displaced or assimilated into the colony.

These early conflicts set a trend for the next century-and-a-half of interaction between Native Americans and English colonists: agreements and accommodations were made early on, often involving mutually beneficial trade; English presence in the area would increase, and their industry or expansion would intensify until they transgressed earlier agreements with the Natives; Natives would either concede or rebuke the colonists, sometimes violently; and finally an armed conflict would unfold that saw the Natives bereft of even more of their land, often while dying of infectious European diseases.

These "American Indian Wars" were rarely more than little conflicts and skirmishes individually, but over the course of the next three hundred years, they would see Native Americans dispossessed of much of their land, as far west as California.

Thanks to the first few decades of this slow but inexorable push against indigenous peoples, English and later British settlers founded the Thirteen Colonies by 1732. These colonies stretched across a huge section of the Atlantic coast and as far west as the Appalachian Mountains.

Native American tribes had their own complex relationships with one another, meanwhile. Many had longstanding alliances with one another or were part of confederations, while others were ancestral enemies. Rival tribes and nations were often played off of one another by French, Spanish, and British colonists in North America so that they would be easier to deal with individually.

This is why in the French and Indian War, the North American theater of the Seven Years' War of 1756-63, both New France and British America called upon Native allies who had hedged their bets with one superpower or the other. Often this was done in the hopes that the colonial ally was less expansionist than their enemy. Alliances didn't usually involve every band in a tribe, though—it was common for many factions to disagree or conflict with one another in a single tribe.

The same kind of splits happened during the American War of Independence, in which over a dozen American Indian tribes fought on behalf of the British Empire or the nascent United States from 1775 to 1783. But Native American tribes lost out both times because French defeat and American victory allowed westward settlement of North America to continue unchecked in the end.

Of the tribes who fight in the American Revolutionary War, four are of great importance for their later roles in the Trail of Tears; the Choctaw and Chickasaw, who fought for the colonists, and the Cherokee and Creek who fought for the British. The tribes generally fought with caution, however. They were protecting their own national sovereignty first and foremost, not getting played like pawns by Europeans.

When the United States secured its independence in 1783, British power was hedged out of North America south of its territories in Canada. Indian policies reoriented accordingly to deal with the expansionist power now growing in the east.

Native & New Americans

Many tribes were dismayed by the defeat of the British. The elimination of British power in the south of North America meant that all of the treaties, alliances, and agreements between Native Americans and the Crown were effectively null and void. At best, the tribes would have to renegotiate terms with the powerful and unchallenged colonists. At worst, as the case often was, they were at the mercy of those newly United States of America.

Talks began as tribes of the American North—and Southeast considered forming a single huge confederation to resist land seizure by the United States. These ideas never turned in to anything concrete; however, and smaller confederations or individual tribes were left to make allies or deal with the U.S. by themselves.

Spain, the only other European power with a strong presence left in North America, was an attractive potential ally to the Creek. These negotiations were also fruitless for the most part because every European empire, including Britain and Spain, agreed to recognize the United States as a legitimate nation.

Many Native Americans refused to acknowledge the legitimacy of the U.S. at first. They were aware of its political coordination and military might, without a doubt. But it was precisely that alien threat posed to Native American sovereignty by this new nation that kept the tribes from acknowledging their new neighbor as properly "American."

The lack of recognition was often mutual over the next thirty years or so. Though U.S. political and military policy toward Native Americans rarely had the express goal of extermination in mind, they were always acting in the interests of the U.S. government or citizens. These interests rarely aligned with those of Natives, so new conflict was inevitable.

The Great Lakes Wars

The American Indian Wars continued to rage periodically with the U.S. at the forefront. The new republic pushed as far west as it could now that it was exempt from old British decrees that kept them out of formerly French land. By 1785, this brought them into conflict with the Native Americans of the Great Lakes Region and the Ohio River, then known as the Northwest Territory.

The Natives of the Great Lakes Region, forming a large Western Confederacy, opposed U.S. encroachment into the area with military force. The Western Confederacy included large Native nations as well as many smaller confederations, totally over thirty different tribes fielding over ten thousand warriors. The confederation was also supplied with firearms by agents in British Canada who wanted to create a Native American bulwark state against the U.S. Handfuls of Natives, mostly Chickasaw and Choctaw, sided with the Euro-American settlers against their old enemies.

The Great Lakes tribes won a series of battles against the inexperienced U.S. militias sent to pacify the region, killing over a thousand of the four thousand-strong force. For most of the war, the Natives were winning. But then in 1792, President George Washington sent the Revolutionary War hero Anthony Wayne to lead a newly reorganized national army and crush the confederation. By 1795, the war was over, and the Ohio Territory was under U.S. occupation.

But the U.S. realized that Britain was supplying arms to the local tribes and agitating them against settlers. This, plus international policies tangled up in the Napoleonic Wars, led the U.S. government to declare war on British holdings in Canada in 1812. The War of 1812 raged until 1815, and once again, both sides called upon their Native allies to help with manpower.

Native Americans from Tecumseh's Confederacy and other groups made up a huge part of Britain's forces early on in the war, and also make up a disproportionately large percentage of the war's death toll. Over ten thousand Native soldiers and civilians were killed by the conflict, and all of the tribes in the Northwest region would lose out on the trade partnerships and support of Britain after the Treaty of Ghent.

Meanwhile, the U.S. was able to continue settling the southern coasts of the Great Lakes with impunity. Local tribes either made concessions to the incoming Euro-Americans or migrated north and west to avoid them. Once again, it seemed that regardless of who won in the wars of European rivalry, Native Americans lost.

Land Purchases

The Northwest Territory might have been the extent of U.S. expansion in the early nineteenth century, had its government not made a bid for a very big stretch of land in

1803. The Louisiana Territory was North American territory formerly occupied by the French. It was ceded to Spain at the conclusion of the French and Indian War, but then in 1800, Spain sold the land back to France.

Napoleon, a consul of the Republic of France at the time, wanted to use Louisiana to recreate a French colonial empire in the Americas. But these dreams were crushed by a renewal of hostilities between France and Britain, as well as the successful Haitian Revolution. With his empire-to-be bleeding money, Napoleon considered selling the land to the United States.

President Thomas Jefferson had wanted to claim the territory for years, so the Louisiana Purchase was soon agreed upon. The territory of the United States practically doubled in size overnight, stretching from the Great Lakes to Louisiana and from Georgia to Montana. For the first time ever, the U.S. had access to the land west of the Mississippi River.

The land was lightly populated, with about 60,000 European and enslaved African inhabitants mostly concentrated in cities and in the south. The Native American population was larger but just as spread out, meaning there were large tracts of "empty" land to develop and use.

And after the conclusion of the War of 1812, the U.S. turned its eyes south toward the Spanish territory of Florida. Florida was the homeland of the Seminole tribe, and so the war that was fought between the U.S. and Spain with its Seminole allies became known as the—First—Seminole War. At its conclusion in the Adams–Onís Treaty of 1819, Spain ceded all of Florida to the United States, opening up more land that would have made for perfect living space, if not for the people already living there.

And the U.S. government knew just what to do about that.

Chapter Two

The "Five Civilized Tribes"

Relations between the U.S. and Native tribes weren't exclusively hostile after the former achieved independence. There was still trade and communication between people, and occasionally a new treaty was made that lasted more than a few years before the United States military inevitably broke it or pursued aggressive re-negotiations.

There was also a surprising amount of cultural diffusion between settlers and indigenous people, going both ways. It is a natural part of different cultures living next to one another. But this cultural exchange was also fostered by what could be called the "humanitarian" elements of Euro-American society. Many citizens of the U.S. abhorred the treatment of Native

Americans, just as they abhorred slavery and other practices of their day.

It was their hope that peace, stability, and a common culture could join their societies together. This "cultural transformation" was a belief espoused by famous historical figures like George Washington and Secretary of War Henry Knox. And by the beginning of the nineteenth century, it felt like a very real possibility.

Unfortunately for Natives, even this well-meaning goal made some steep demands of their tribes. It wasn't a policy of equality, cultural diversity, or making a hybrid culture. It was a policy of acculturating and then fully assimilating Native Americans into white American society, which those white Americans generally saw as superior.

Amazingly, this was still a fairly progressive idea for the time, because it still held that Natives were equally human to Europeans—an idea that was not at all universal in the eighteenth and nineteenth centuries.

Such ideas as Christianity, industrialization, centralized governments, literacy, participation in the free capitalist market, and even the practice of plantation farming using African slaves were exported by the U.S. to the larger tribes of the American Southeast. There was also a tacit approval of intermarriage between whites and Native Americans. In essence, the goal was to "whiten the Indian" until they became U.S. citizens, at which point the land wars would end.

Most Native American tribes weren't very keen to lose the ways of life they had literally been fighting and dying to protect for centuries. But that didn't mean that some tribes didn't decide to pick and choose. Pragmatic, adaptive people took on some or all of these elements of Euro-American culture in order to meet the needs of their changing world, while also protecting the rest of their societies.

This led to the recognition of some Native tribes as being more "civilized"—read: more like Europeans—in the eyes of the United States. The hybridized tribes in the American Southeast became known as the "Five Civilized Tribes", and the federal government often recognized their sovereignty even as state borders expanded to surround their lands. These tribes were the Cherokee, the Choctaw, the Chickasaw, the Seminole, and the Muscogee, who are more commonly called the Creek.

Mississippian Inheritors

Of course, the Five Tribes were already civilized, even before coming in to contact with European settlers. Civilization is a *highly* subjective term.

The Five Tribes were descendants of, or were at least very influenced by, the old Mississippian Culture that thrived in the South between the ninth and sixteenth centuries. This culture farmed maize intensively, built earthen pyramids, worked metals like copper, had complex political and religious systems, and developed cities that covered hundreds of acres and contained thousands of people.

Their culture declined for several reasons and didn't survive contact with the first Europeans explorers. They left no written accounts, but their archaeological record is rich. What many people mistake for hills along the Mississippi River today are, in fact, the remains of their ancient pyramids.

The Mississippian peoples didn't just die out when their society ended, though. They divided and joined or became different cultural groups over time, eventually giving rise to the Choctaw, Chickasaw, Creek, and Seminole nations. These four tribes spoke related languages from the area. The Cherokee migrated down from the Appalachians around the sixteenth century and spoke an Iroquoian language, but they still spent enough time in the cultural area to be influenced by it.

These tribes inherited many complex traditions from the old Mississippians, and had their own unique innovations, long before they began to accept and adapt European customs. But the new ideas did have their uses. By taking English names, converting to Christianity—or at least mixing it with their indigenous beliefs—and sometimes sharing in the slave trade, the Five Tribes ingratiated themselves to their European neighbors.

As a result, the relations between the U.S. and the Five Tribes became much more developed than those the U.S. had with other "savage" tribes. Up until the 1820s, they were allowed to operate as autonomous nations within U.S. borders. They were ultimately beholden to the federal government, but had full internal control of their nations. And for a time, this was enough.

Tribe vs State Rights

But the population was booming in American cities along the east coast, and slavery was expanding in the South. Cotton cultivation was approaching its zenith, and the recently invented cotton gin made farming huge tracts of the crop even easier. Euro-Americans needed more land to keep up with their rapid growth, and Native American land was often the target.

While the relationship between the tribes and the U.S. federal government could be amicable, the relationships between tribes and *state* governments often were not. This was an era of U.S. history where the battle between state rights and central government authority was still raging—and it would only grow worse until the outbreak of the American Civil War later that century.

State governments often allowed their citizens to squat on tribal territory, building unofficial settlements on land they didn't own. Sometimes this was state policy, sometimes the government just turned a blind eye when its citizens did it on their own. When tribal governments took issue with this, the matter was brought to state courts, where Native Americans rarely received equal representation.

Natives were not considered U.S. citizens, except in cases where their land had just been officially annexed and they had the "option" to assimilate. Therefore, state courts rarely ruled in their favor, and tribal lands were slowly chipped away at from all sides over the decades.

They tried appealing to the Supreme Court on occasion, but the result was usually that the federal government was unwilling to infringe upon state business, for fear of stepping on too many toes. It would also be especially unpopular for the government to meddle in support of a group that was seen as an outsider.

Eventually, a firmer decision was handed down in the 1823 case of Johnson v. McIntosh. This ruling stated that while Native Americans could occupy and control lands inside the United States, they couldn't hold actual titles to those lands. This made it even harder for tribes to assert their land rights, allowing squatting and *de facto* annexation to continue.

After the Louisiana and Florida Purchases, some U.S. statesmen began to talk of removing all of the southeastern Native tribes—including the Five Tribes—and sending them west of the Mississippi River to populate the empty, less desirable land there. This would open their old land up to white settlers for good, and allow the U.S. to establish stronger control over the tribes. This "Indian Territory" would be a designated homeland—one of the first reservations—for tens of thousands of Native Americans.

The next decade would be spent formulating exactly how to do that, while also trying to convince the country that it was a good idea.

Chapter Three

The Indian Removal Act of 1830

There is one person who can be pointed out as more responsible for passing Indian Removal legislation than anyone else, and that is Andrew Jackson.

(Source: https://en.wikipedia.org/wiki/File:Andrew_jackson_headFXD.jpg)

Andrew Jackson was a soldier before he became the seventh President of the United States in 1829. He fought in the War of 1812, and the First Seminole War, both of which saw him commanding troops against the British and Spanish, as well as many of their respective Native American allies. His toughness and steely resolve in the face of those bitter battles earned him the nickname "Old Hickory."

For more than a decade before he took office, Jackson was of the opinion that Native Americans should be removed from their current situation in lands east of the Mississippi. Jackson was a strict Federalist and believed that the existence of autonomous tribal nations inside U.S. territory was an unconstitutional violation of state sovereignty. In particular he saw it as going against Article IV, Section 3 of the Constitution which contains a property clause that reads:

"The Congress shall have Power to dispose of and make all needful Rules and Regulations respecting the Territory or other Property belonging to the United States; and nothing in this Constitution shall be so construed as to Prejudice any Claims of the United States, or of any particular State."

In Jackson's mind, Native Americans could coexist with the United States by taking one of two choices: either give up sovereignty, gain citizenship, and assimilate to state laws; or relinquish their lands in return for a piece of Indian Territory where they could enjoy more limited self-governance.

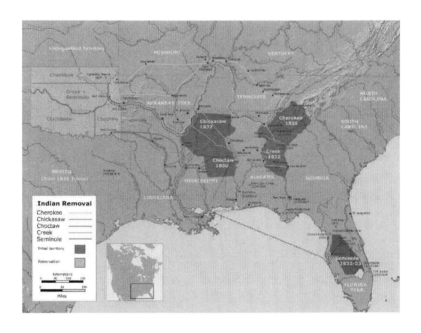

(Source: https://commons.wikimedia.org/wiki/File:Trails_of_Tears_en.png)

One of the greatest shames of the Trail of Tears era is that the citizenship alternative rarely protected the Native Americans. The government forces who oversaw migration or forced Removal were often made up of militias drawn from nearby states, or territories seeking to achieve statehood.

These militia members often had personal, political, or economic incentives to remove as many Natives as they could.

These militias discriminated against the rights of non-white citizens, who could rarely present their cases in court thanks to the hostility of state governments and the inaction of the federal government and Supreme Court. Citizens of Native American descent were driven out of annexed territory and onto the shrinking plots still clung to by their tribes, even if they had the means to prove their citizenship.

This point bears repeating. The United States of America effectively rounded up and then deported its own citizens. It subjected them to hardship and death on the basis of their ethnicity so that another group could profit from their misfortune.

And it would only get worse from here.

Support for the Act

After eight years of ugly, mud-slinging campaigning with John Quincy Adams that saw the death of Andrew's wife Rachel and the destruction of the nonpartisan Era of Good Feelings, Jackson was elected President. His campaign partly ran on the promise of "Indian Removal" and he even included it in his inaugural address.

The rhetoric for Removal included *all* Native Americans within U.S. borders at this point, including the Five Civilized Tribes. According to Jackson it was "God's will" that the land be developed and not left "idle" in the hands of Native Americans. Manifest Destiny at its finest.

Yet it also seems that Jackson and some of his supporters sincerely believed that relocation of Natives was a wise and even humane decision. While it is easy today to see that as a cover for greed and bigotry, there was unfortunately a sliver of truth to it. Racism abounded in those days, and entire tribes had already been violently wiped out in the south as well as the north.

The Cherokee, largest of the Five Tribes, was, at the time, locked in a bitter legal dispute over their lands with the state of Georgia, which was one of the largest and most powerful states in the Union at that time. If a resolution to the land dispute didn't come soon, a military conflict that the Cherokee couldn't hope to win was likely to break out.

By arguing that the decline of Native Americans was inevitable in the face of civilization and progress, relocation became an attractive alternative. By relocating the tribes west, they would be "spared" from certain annihilation while also speeding up the progress that threatened them to begin with.

And by espousing this circular argument, Jackson and his supporters could rely on the myth of the "Vanishing Indian" to support their argument while simultaneously reinforcing the myth. Congressional support for an Indian Removal Act grew strong, but its opponents were just as strong at first.

There were, of course, simple economic incentives, as well. The United States would receive almost three million immigrants between 1820 and 1850, and this much bigger population made land and space to live in that much more valuable. A brutally pragmatic "us or them" thought process decided who would get that land, and made many ordinary U.S. citizens see Indian Removal as a good thing.

Opposition to the Act

Because the Five Tribes were located in what would become the Deep South, wealthy slave-owners were big supporters of a Removal Act. The land taken from the Natives in that way would add to the territories of slaveholder states, empowering the South and its uniting interests. Conversely, people opposed to slavery—generally in the North—largely opposed Removal. Enemies of President Jackson in the north *or* south also tended to oppose the Act.

In addition to not wanting their ideological rivals to get stronger, Northerners and abolitionists opposed Indian Removal on moral grounds. According to countless Protestant churches and missionary workers working to assimilate the tribes, it was an abominable and unchristian thing to do.

Reformers and Native American rights activists like Jeremiah Evarts fought to gather up enough "friendly" congressmen to oppose the bill. He was a close friend to the Cherokee, and believed that peaceful, voluntary assimilation could happen if time were allowed.

In response, the state of Georgia enacted a law in 1830, that prohibited whites like him from living on Cherokee land after March 31, 1831. This was meant to deliberately hamstring his social work. Evarts overworked himself to death with tuberculosis the following year, dealing a terrible blow to the missionary opposition to Indian Removal.

New Jersey Senator Theodore Frelinghuysen was another bitter opponent of the Act. In response to Jackson's "laws of nature" argument that God intended for the land to be exploited to its fullest, Frelinghuysen pointed out that the U.S.

government had not even finished selling the land it had previously confiscated from tribal nations.

He was wrong in calculating that it would take another two hundred years to sell it all to settlers, but he did expose how the illegal practices of squatting and encroachment were fueling the bill, rather than legitimate land purchases.

Most famous among opponents to the Indian Removal Act was Davy Crockett. The statesman and frontiersman from Tennessee opposed the bill in Congress, and was the only representative from his state to do so. He did this both because of the moral issue he saw in taking ancestral lands away from their people, and because he had a deep personal divide with Andrew Jackson, his former general.

Opposing the bill—and Jackson—greatly damaged Crockett's political career back home, and he found reelection harder and harder until he was effectively blacklisted by his own district in 1835. This turn of events led to him to setting off west with his band of revolutionaries to fight in the territory of Texas, and ultimately, die at the Alamo.

Passage of the Indian Removal Act

The lines were drawn in the sand for months before a vote on the Act was held. When the vote began in April 1830, the fighting was fiercest. In the end, the Senate passed the bill on April 24, with a conclusive vote of twenty-eight to nineteen. It wasn't until May 26, that the House of Representatives passed the bill by the much narrower margin of one hundred and two to ninety-seven votes.

President Andrew Jackson signed the Indian Removal Act in to law on May 28, 1830. The finalized draft of the Act authorized him, as President, to negotiate treaties of Removal with Native American tribes in U.S. territory, giving them federal land west of the Mississippi in exchange for their ancestral homelands east of it.

The tribes would have their migrations paid for, and government appraisers would also pay the Natives for anything of value left behind in the east. The Act also promised that the new lands in the west would belong to them "forever," and that the U.S. government and military would subsidize their first year and protect the Native Americans from any hostile groups, Native or white. Delivering on these promises would be harder than making them, of course.

Implementation of the Act

Native American leaders were summoned almost immediately to negotiate treaties. Talks were to be held at the Franklin, Tennessee, residence of the Secretary of War, John Eaton, in May 1830. Invitations were sent to four of the Five Tribes, excluding the Seminoles who were on Jackson's agenda, but who were too out of the way in their Floridian swamps to focus on removing yet. Jackson attended the talks personally, expecting swift and easy negotiations.

No one but the Chickasaws bothered showing up, and they only came to drive a very hard bargain against Jackson and Eaton. The rest of the leaders of their respective tribes were almost entirely against relocating, counter to Jackson's expectation that they would have had enough intrusion, discrimination, and harassment from Anglo-American settlers by now.

An agreement was reached between Jackson and the Chickasaw, but it hinged on the Chickasaw finding western land that they deemed suitable. The deal proceeded to fall through several times as Chickasaw rangers came back dissatisfied with their findings in Indian Territory. This would prolong the tension between the two parties, but it ensured that the Chickasaw would not be the first tribe removed from its home.

Chapter Four

Choctaw Removal

The dubious honor of being the first tribe pushed to Removal went to the Choctaw of modern-day northern Mississippi and western Alabama. The Choctaw, who were steadfast allies of the United States in many conflicts such as the Creek War, had signed eight treaties with the U.S. government between 1786 and 1825.

Seven of these treaties ceded a total of almost fifteen million acres of land to the States. One last treaty signed on September 27, 1830, would raise that acreage to nearly twenty-five million, selling all of their remaining lands east of the Mississippi.

This was the Treaty of Dancing Rabbit Creek, negotiated by Secretary Eaton and several Choctaw chiefs including Greenwood LeFlore. LeFlore was a mixed-race man with a high-ranking Choctaw mother and a French-Canadian fur trader. In many ways he was an exemplar of the ideal of Native American cultural transformation held by whites: he was a political reformer, Christian, European-educated, and convinced of the inevitability of Euro-American supremacy.

LeFlore was unpopular with the full-blooded traditionalists of his nation, but after the passing of the Indian Removal Act, he found himself elevated to principal chief of the Choctaws, thanks to a series of angry resignations by other chiefs. He wielded more individual authority than any other chief up to that point, and he was going to use it to secure the best possible future for his people.

The Choctaw nation had gotten some land west of the Mississippi from the earlier treaty of Doak's Stand in 1820, and a small number of Choctaws had voluntarily settled there over the years. The plan now was to convince the rest of the tribe to do so as quickly and as smoothly as possible; therefore, creating a blueprint for President Jackson and his successors to follow for all future Removals. LeFlore seemed like the perfect agent to meet them halfway for this.

After the failed Franklin Talks brought Secretary Eaton and Colonel John Coffee to Choctaw land, LeFlore hosted them to a two-week long event that resembled a carnival. He used his personal charisma to its full extent during the talks, and negotiated in front of an audience of six thousand of his tribe members. The treaty was signed by Eaton, Coffee, LeFlore, two other Choctaw chiefs, Mushulatubbee, and Nittucachee, and over two hundred other observers.

Twenty-two terms were agreed upon in the final draft of the treaty. Among them were promises for the ceding of all eastern Choctaw lands in return for fifteen million acres in Indian Territory, autonomy of this new western Choctaw nation forever, payment for transportation as well as the construction of schools and other community buildings, and food, and annuities to help establish the new nation.

The treaty also offered significant opportunities for those Choctaws unwilling to leave their homeland. Allotments of land, now owned by the U.S. government, were to be given to any Choctaw on which to settle and practice Euro-American style agriculture. Each family would be given about six hundred and forty acres each. The remaining Natives would also be given a path to full U.S. citizenship and assimilation.

This was the closest to the best of both worlds that LeFlore believed he could secure for his tribe. The treaty was divisive among Choctaws, some of whom believed that LeFlore gave in too easily to pressure to resettle west. Others saw his actions as necessary pragmatism, and were grateful for unifying the Choctaw and securing for them the largest area of land that would ever be given to a tribe in Indian Territory.

(Source:
https://commons.wikimedia.org/wiki/File:Flag_of_the_Choctaw_Nation.PNG)

Unfortunately, LeFlore's legacy is tarnished by several unfortunate realities. First, is the fact that the treaty he sacrificed so much for was not entirely respected by the U.S. government or its agents. William Ward, the agent assigned to the Choctaw allotment case, made it as difficult as he could for Natives to receive land and citizenship, deliberately violating the spirit and the letter of the agreement. The heads of large families were discriminated against, meaning that only small groups of Choctaws totaling less than seventy people were permitted to stay.

Incidentally, LeFlore and his family members were among those lucky enough to gain an allotment, and LeFlore chose to stay behind in the east to pursue citizenship rather than make the harsh trek west with the majority of his people. He lived a relatively comfortable life in Mississippi, and was even elected as a state representative and senator in the 1840s, where he became a close friend of future Confederate President Jefferson Davis.

While he lived like this, LeFlore sent a small group of Choctaws west even before the Dancing Rabbit treaty was ratified the following year. LeFlore boasted to President Jackson that he could have gotten his tribe to migrate even without the treaty, and seemed to want to speed the process up while also demonstrating his own ability as a leader.

This trial Removal was an almost complete failure. Of the one thousand-strong Choctaw vanguard that left in late 1830, only eighty-eight survived the five-hundred-and-fifty-mile trek to Indian Territory. Those who made it were on the verge of starvation.

LeFlore's reputation was damaged by this, and later in 1830, Mushulatubbee reasserted his power as elected chief of the western division of the Choctaws, reducing LeFlore's centralized authority. In October 1830, LeFlore was deposed by the national Choctaw council in favor of his maternal nephew, George H. Harkins.

Shortly before the first wave of expulsion began, Harkins wrote the famously bittersweet "Farewell Letter to the American People." In this widely published open letter, he meditated upon the abuses his people had suffered, while wishing nothing but the best for the state of Mississippi, and for future relations between Native and Euro-American peoples.

Harkins, Mushulatubbee, and other chiefs would lead the Choctaw through their mandated migrations, but it would not be enough to avoid the worst luck or abuses.

Choctaw Removal Begins

The rest of the Choctaw people were set to begin the process of Removal in autumn of 1831, several months after the treaty was ratified in February 24. But the first Choctaws traveling west according to treaty regulations quickly discovered that U.S. aid would be either insufficient or nonexistent.

Mismanagement of the migration could be felt immediately in the cold air around them. The first group of Choctaws was ordered by their overseer George Gaines to begin their journey on November 1, which would leave them exposed to the dead of winter in the middle of their slow trip either on foot or riding slow, heavy wagons.

The plan was for departing Choctaws to gather in to two large groups at the cities of Memphis and Vicksburg, where they would travel west by land. But the winter of '31 was brutal, and stopped the Choctaws in their tracks with sleet, snow, and the occasional flash flood which made further wagon transport impossible.

Then, the emigrants began to run low on food. The citizens of Vicksburg and Memphis were worried about the strain of feeding all of the Natives for the winter, so a group of steamboats was requisitioned to ferry them across the rivers.

The Memphis group walked sixty miles along the Arkansas river to a port, only to be stuck waiting in the cold for weeks while ice choked the harbor. Extreme food rationing saw every person eating less than a handful of boiled corn and a single turnip per day. Even water was rationed to two cups a day because the frozen river water was so difficult to thaw. Meanwhile, the Vicksburg group couldn't even find the rivers at first, and were led through inhospitable swamps around Lake Providence, Louisiana by incompetent guides.

Eventually government wagons were sent to pick the Choctaws up and bring them to Little Rock, Arkansas, where the first recorded reference to the Removal as "a trail of tears and death" was uttered by a distraught Choctaw chief. Both groups eventually reached Fort Towson, the U.S. army outpost built to protect the southern border of Indian Territory from the former Spanish colonies in the south.

Upon reaching Fort Towson, the first wave of Choctaw migrants had effectively reached their new home. They would barely have a year to organize their new settlements before the second wave set out in 1832.

The second wave followed the same route as the first, and experienced less harsh weather despite traveling at approximately the same time of year. Unfortunately, the wave's lack of deaths by exposure was made up for by a severe outbreak of cholera, killing many.

The third and final wave of Choctaw migrants in 1833, was the least lethal of them all, but by no means free of casualties. Fifteen thousand Choctaws and a few hundred African slaves departed for Indian Territory over the span of two-and-a-half years, and between two and five thousand of them died on the trek west. The wide range of possible deaths with no official death toll attests to how little government oversight the Choctaw Removal had.

Aftermath

One reason for the lack of U.S. government support on the brutal, five-month journey undertaken by the Choctaw people was the cost. The government was surprised to find that it had greatly underestimated the resources needed to transport so many people in such a short time. The new price range was two to three times the original estimate.

In an era of volatile relationships between states and the federal government, higher taxes to cover the expenses of the Indian Removal Act truly could have led to civil war. So, taxes were avoided for the most part, and the price was paid in blood, sweat, and tears by the Choctaw tribe.

After the first waves of Removal proved so disastrous, many Choctaws became even more determined to stay.

Reduced to squatters in their own homeland, between five and six thousand Choctaws refused the Treaty of Dancing Rabbit Creek deadline and stayed in what was now Mississippi.

These Mississippi Choctaws would face legal and physical harassment for decades to come. White settlers attacked them and destroyed their homes and property to try and drive the Choctaw out for good. This resulted in a slow stream of refugees fleeing west until the beginning of the twentieth century.

With up to a third of the Choctaw nation dead or stranded in Mississippi, the first chapter of Indian Removal might seem like a failure. But President Jackson was looking for a model to follow for all other Removals, and at the very least the Choctaw Removal had succeeded in freeing up land for Euro-American settlers.

In that respect, the expulsion of the Choctaw was considered enough of a success to mimic for all subsequent Removals. Thousands of people were dead, and thousands more were likely to follow. The migrations had *already* come to be known as the Trail of Tears, yet the U.S. government would carry on with this new business as usual.

Chapter Five

Seminole Removal

The Seminoles were a tribe that the U.S. had been dealing with domestically since only very recent times. The Adams–Onís Treaty of 1821 granted the U.S. access to the Territory of Florida, homeland of the Seminoles. The tribe had a warlike reputation among Euro-Americans after allying with Spain against the U.S., though they were still counted among the Five Civilized Tribes for many cultural practices they had.

The tribe generally lived so deep in the wetland reservation given to them by the 1823 Treaty of Moultrie Creek that contact was difficult, unneeded, and mostly unwanted. But eventually Seminoles started hunting and grazing beyond the legal borders of their reservation because the land they'd been given was unlivable for their numbers.

This alarmed wealthy Floridian planters, and sped up government response. It took until 1832 for the U.S. government to reach out and speak to the tribe about the prospect of Removal.

The U.S. Department of War appointed James Gadsden as commissioner and sent him to meet with a delegation of Seminole chiefs at Payne's Landing on the Ocklawaha River in spring of 1832. Because of the staunch opposition that many Seminoles were expected to have toward migrating to Indian Territory, the meeting was clandestine and almost-secret.

The meeting was also mired in snags as the assembled chiefs refused to accept Gadsden's offered terms. His terms were similar to those offered to the Choctaws in that the Seminoles would give up all of their ancestral land and migrate to Indian Territory within three years.

But instead of establishing their own nation the Seminole tribe would be merged with the small number of Creek—Muscogee—people who had moved there prior to the passing of the Indian Removal Act.

The logic behind this was that the Seminole was an offshoot of the Creek, rather than a tribe unto itself. And while there was a cultural and linguistic link between the Creek and some of the bands of the Seminole thanks to their shared Mississippian Culture influence, there was no shared sense of *identity* between the two peoples. So, the Seminoles did not agree with this idea, and refused.

(Source: https://commons.wikimedia.org/wiki/File:Flag_of_the_Seminole_Tribe_of_Florida.PNG)

Another contentious point asked by Gadsden was for the Seminole tribe to give up all of its runaway slaves, whom Southern planters feared in great numbers. While the Seminoles were known to keep African slaves, their conditions were very different from those seen in plantation chattel slavery.

Oftentimes, slaves worked and lived as members of Seminole families, and could rise to powerful and important positions in a group. This more accepting attitude, therefore, made Seminole territory an attractive destination for runaway slaves from elsewhere in the American South.

As a result, the Seminole tribe boasted large numbers of runaway slaves and freedmen in their communities. There was also a class of entirely free mixed-race "Black Seminoles" that came from their frequent intermarriage. The Seminoles were not about to essentially hand over their own people, so on that point they also refused.

Somehow, the treaty was still negotiated. There is no written account of how a draft was agreed upon, by participants or witnesses, but evidently a group of seven Seminole chiefs agreed to act as land surveyors in Indian Territory. If they determined that the land was good enough, they would agree to the treaty and the tribe would move. The Treaty of Payne's Landing was signed on May 9, 1832.

In October of that year, the chiefs departed for Indian Territory. They were aware of how different the climate was from Florida's, and they spent a large amount of time meeting with the nearby Creek who had lived on the land for years by that point. Supposedly, the Seminoles signed a statement confirming their agreement with the treaty at Fort Gibson on March 28, 1833.

This is "supposed," because when the Seminole delegation returned to Florida, they denied having ever signed a document like that, or else claimed that they had been forced to sign it against their will.

This was exacerbated by the fact that many Seminole chiefs were not literate enough to write their own names, and so signed the treaty and/or the document with only an "X" mark, which could have been more easily falsified than a personal signature.

But even if they had signed the document, they were only seven headsmen, and their word was not enough to convince thousands of Seminoles spread across dozens of bands. The tribe thus refused the entire treaty, while the U.S. government believed it to be effective and binding. The three-year countdown for Removal began, and the Seminoles tried to wait out the clock.

Not all of the Seminole people lived on the reservation at this time. There was a small number of them who had been permitted by the Treaty of Moultrie Creek to remain on and around the Apalachicola River in the north. They were isolated from the rest of the Seminole nation as a result.

This made the northern Seminoles easier to persuade to travel west after years of harassment from settlers, and in 1834, they did so. The trek was fairly bloodless because of how small the group was. But it was still a difficult journey, especially with several hundred miles added on compared to what the Choctaws had walked years prior. The death toll would pale in comparison to what was to come.

Tensions Rise

After becoming convinced by the migration of the northern Seminoles that Removal was possible, the U.S. government ratified the Treaty of Payne's Landing in April 1834. But the time limit before the Seminoles had to be gone was still counting down, and they were expected to leave in 1835. To speed up migration, the U.S. sent a new agent to deal with the tribe.

Wiley Thompson arrived at Fort King in northern Florida in October 1834, and called the Seminole chiefs together to persuade them to leave. The Seminoles again refused to leave their homes, and reiterated that the treaty, of which there were no negotiation records, felt illegitimate to them. In response,

Thompson called for military reinforcements at Forts King and Brooke.

The Seminoles had obtained their annuity payment from the treaty, at least according to Thompson, and used the money to stockpile gunpowder and shot. With a more substantial U.S. army presence in Fort King, Thompson tried assembling the chiefs again in March of 1835. This time, he read aloud a letter from President Jackson addressed to them.

Andrew Jackson, who had fought against the Seminoles in the War of 1812, had a very low standing in the eyes of the tribe. But his fierce military prowess was remembered all too well, and the threat of force personally made in his letter seemed to sway the chiefs. They asked to have one month to debate and respond, which was granted.

The next month, the Seminoles once again said that they would not be moving west. Agent Thompson was rather annoyed by this point, and a fight reportedly broke out between him and the chiefs that had to be stopped by General Clinch of Fort Garrison before violence erupted. Five prominent chiefs including Micanopy of the Alachua Seminoles still refused, but eight agreed and asked to delay the move until the end of 1835. An exasperated Thompson agreed.

While he waited for the extension to run out, Thompson set about dealing with the five chiefs who had refused Removal. Despite having no authority in Seminole government, Thompson declared that those chiefs had lost their positions. This in turn ruined Seminole relations to the point that not even the eight chiefs entertained leaving any longer.

The government then issued a ban on the sale of all guns and ammunition to the Seminoles. This enraged many Seminoles, including a hot-blooded young warrior named Osceola. Osceola compared the ban to Americans trying to turn his people "black" which is to say, make them like slaves.

Osceola then started to cause trouble around Fort King, for which he was imprisoned. Thompson attempted to be more diplomatic then, securing Osceola's release and attempting to befriend him. He even gifted him a rifle, and in return Osceola claimed he would bring his followers back to the fort where he would abide by the treaty.

On his way back up to Fort King, Osceola heard of the escalating violence between Seminoles and white settlers. Small attacks were being made by both sides, resulting in a handful of injuries and one dead Seminole, as well as a dead

U.S. mail courier whom Dalton, Georgia, would later be named after. Osceola also encountered Chief Charley Emathla, who saw a war coming and wanted no part in it, so he was bringing his band to Fort Brooke where they would board ships bound for the west.

Osceola murdered Emathla for his perceived betrayal and cowardice, worsening the situation. By this point, the U.S. garrison in Florida realized how resistant the Seminoles would be, and started to mobilize a proper army for war. Small skirmishes broke out between U.S. militias and Seminole war parties as farms were raided and towns burned. By December 1835, it was feared that Fort King would be overrun by Seminoles so two companies under Major Francis L. Dade were sent to reinforce it.

The reinforcements never arrived.

On December 23, Dade's column of one hundred and ten soldiers was ambushed by Chief Micanopy and one hundred and eighty of his warriors, who had been stalking them for days. Dade died in the first volley, and all but three of his men were killed in the ensuing battle.

Osceola would have partaken in the battle, but he and his men were too busy murdering Agent Wiley Thompson at Fort

King, possibly with the rifle he had given him. Upon hearing of this, General Clinch came down from Fort Drane with seven hundred and fifty soldiers, mostly volunteers. The Second Seminole War had begun.

The Second Seminole War and Consequences

The war was a miserable, almost decade-long affair that saw atrocities and loss of civilian life on both sides. There were truces, reversals, false flag operations, and further massacres. At least one thousand U.S. soldiers were killed, mostly from disease, as well as an unknown number of Euro-American settlers. Alongside them were almost three thousand Seminoles, Black Seminoles, and runaway slaves, who were not always distinguished between warriors and noncombatants by the enemy.

Transportation began even before the war's end on August 14, 1842. Seminoles were sent west as prisoners of war, rather than as reluctant emigrants like many other Native Americans on the Trail of Tears. As many as four thousand Seminoles were made to board ships in western Florida, sail to port cities in Louisiana such as New Orleans, and then march north to Indian Territory over the span of the war.

Disease and starvation caused by the war killed many of these emigrants. Famously, a chieftain named Tiger Tail did not surrender until the last battle in the entire war, holding out despite being on the verge of death from some unknown disease. He had to be carried on a litter to meet with the U.S. army and arrange for his people's transportation west. He died in New Orleans in 1843, reportedly committing a defiant suicide by swallowing powdered glass.

Seminoles were settled on Creek land as the Treaty of Payne's Landing stated. This created a lot of tension between the two groups, partly because of the relatively large number of Creek slave-owners living so close to free or formerly enslaved Black Seminoles. Despite these problems, they could not split their land and the U.S. government considered the two separate tribes to be a single tribal nation.

Not all of the Seminoles left Florida, however. The fighting spirit of some bands was too strong to break, and their hideouts in the everglades were too hard to find. Eventually the U.S. army afforded them a much smaller impromptu reservation in southwest Florida so that the enormously expensive war could end.

Floridian Seminoles, who boast that they never surrendered or signed a treaty with the United States, numbered in the low-to-mid hundreds by the end of the century.

Chapter Six

Creek Removal

The Creeks, whom the Seminoles were forced to settle with in the 1840s, had already been present in Indian Territory since, at least, 1826. The series of events that brought them there, and would continue to send Creeks west, was a long chain of broken treaties, as well as an unexpected success or two.

As a consequence of British influence during the War of 1812, the Creek nation became embroiled in civil war that spilled out in to a general war involving the United States. The rebelling faction, a group of younger Upper Creeks known as "Red Sticks" for their painted war clubs, wanted to end U.S. influence and "civilizing programs" influencing the Creek tribe.

The Red Sticks were inspired by the Shawnee leader Tecumseh, who led a large tribal confederation during the War of 1812. They mostly kept their anti-U.S. agenda a secret, until an episode of violence in February of 1813, where a band of Red Sticks murdered two families of white settlers close to Nashville, Tennessee.

Benjamin Hawkins, the Indian Agent associated with the Creek tribe, demanded that the Red Sticks war party be handed over to the authorities. Instead, the Creek National Council had them executed according to their own law. This angered U.S. authorities and caused the war to expand in scope until the Red Sticks faction surrendered in 1814, by the U.S. army and allied Creeks.

Andrew Jackson, still a General at the time, held the entire Creek nation accountable for the Red Sticks rebellion, and went so far as to blame them for not killing Tecumseh sooner during the War of 1812. The Treaty of Fort Jackson, which he oversaw the signing of reflected this general disdain, requiring that the entire tribe cede over twenty million acres of land to the United States.

This was more than half of the tribe's homeland, and its annexation by the states of Alabama and Georgia caused many

Red Stick Creeks to flee south in to Florida, where they'd join the Seminoles in their later resistance against the United States. Other Creeks crowded in to their reduced territory and begrudgingly continued to offer occasional military aid to the U.S., such as in the Seminole Wars.

McIntosh & Indian Springs

In the late 1810s a Creek chieftain named William McIntosh—unrelated to the case of Johnson vs. M'Intosh—rose to prominence. Similar to Greenwood LeFlore of the Choctaw, McIntosh was a mixed-race man who gained his office partly because of his high-ranking mother. He was also a reformer who took steps to centralize his tribe's government, going so far as to create a police force known as the Law Menders.

Also, like LeFlore, McIntosh eventually considered forced migration to be inevitable for Native Americans, and tried to prepare his tribe for it. This led to him signing the First and Second Treaty of Indian Springs in the early 1820s.

The First Treaty of Indian Springs came from multiple angles of pressure being put on the Creeks. The state of Georgia, led by Governor George Troup wanted the Creeks to cede land bordering on Cherokee territory so that they would be split and unable to form a military alliance with one another.

The citizens of Georgia also lodged three hundred and fifty thousand dollars in unpaid claims against the Creeks arising from trade debts—a number that was probably inflated—and wanted them settled. Finally, the U.S. government wanted to kick-start Creek emigration, even before the Indian Removal Act passed.

The treaty, signed by McIntosh, ceded around four million acres of land to Georgia, completely annexing all Creek land east of the Flint River on December 8, 1821. In return, the federal government agreed to pay the Creek nation two hundred thousand dollars over the next fourteen years, as well as pay the people of Georgia for any debts the Creeks did have with them.

Yet again painting similarities between LeFlore and McIntosh is the fact that McIntosh made off unusually well from the treaty. The government paid him forty thousand dollars and secured one thousand acres for him personally, much the same as how LeFlore was able to enjoy the difficult-to-earn benefits of citizenship from the Treaty of Dancing Rabbit Creek.

McIntosh built a luxurious hotel on the land, which attracted the attention of more wealthy whites, which intensified state efforts to take more land from the Creeks. This in turn led the Creek National Council to pass a law stating that any further ceding of land to the United States would be punishable by death.

Undeterred, McIntosh led six other chiefs to negotiate the Second Treaty of Indian Springs with the government at his hotel on February 12, 1825. This treaty ceded to the state of Georgia everything east of the Chattahoochee River, which was by now the vast majority of remaining Creek land. It even gave away the Ocmulgee area, which was a sacred site of ritual, as well as the home to several ancient mounds from the Mississippian Culture.

Again, the Creek would receive installments of money totaling up to two hundred thousand dollars, but this time the money was to be used to facilitate the Creek migrating west to land on the Arkansas River at some indeterminate point in the future.

McIntosh received another direct payment from the U.S. in this treaty—the whopping sum of two hundred thousand dollars up front, mirroring what his entire tribe was supposed

71

to get over the next decade. It may come as no surprise that Chief McIntosh and Governor Troup, the two biggest forces behind both of these treaties, happened to be first cousins.

The treaty was signed, as was McIntosh's death warrant. The Creek people were outraged, and the National Council denounced it before calling for McIntosh and the other signatories to be executed, as the 1821 law required.

On April 29, 1825, the Upper Creek chief Menawa brought over two hundred warriors with him to McIntosh's wealthy plantation located on his private reserve. William McIntosh and two of the six chiefs were killed, the house was burned to the ground, and both of McIntosh's sons-in-law were taken to be executed, though one escaped.

The Creeks go to Washington

In the wake of this bloodshed the Creek National Council sent a delegation led by chief Opothleyahola to Washington, D.C. They petitioned President John Quincy Adams, who was far more sympathetic to Native Americans than his successor would be. President Adams was persuaded, and for the first time in American history a treaty was renegotiated in order to be more advantageous to a Native American party.

The Treaty of Washington still ceded many tracts of Creek land east of Chattahoochee to Georgia, but it spared a portion and kept the sacred Ocmulgee grounds in Creek hands. It also raised the payment to two hundred and seventeen thousand and six hundred dollars while condensing it in to a one-time payment upfront. Additionally, the Creek nation would receive a twenty-thousand-dollar annuity from that point on.

The treaty also took steps to mend the internal damage done to the Creek Nation. Signers of the Treaties of Indian Springs, as well as Lower Creeks once led by McIntosh, would be guaranteed the same rights and privileges as the Creeks signing this new treaty. Furthermore, damages were paid by the U.S. government to cover the infighting which had broken out surrounding McIntosh's death.

On top of this, the non-obligatory option of relocation west of the Mississippi was offered, again to be paid by the U.S. government, which would also aid any migrating Creeks establish their new territory, including providing them with utilities, interpreters, and a federal Indian Agent.

The Treaty of Washington was signed on January 24, 1826. All in all, it was still detrimental to the Creeks staying in their ancestral homeland, but it did equip the tribe with far better means to survive a radical transition like leaving it. And in view of the long and unfair history of Native American treaties, that much was cause for celebration.

Naturally, it would be struck down.

(Source: https://commons.wikimedia.org/wiki/File:Muscogee_Nation_Seal.png)

Despite all of the pressure put on him to stop white settlers from encroaching on Creek land, Governor Troup faced even greater pressure from his own expansionist constituents. He was unhappy with the Treaty of Washington and refused to agree to it. Instead, he ordered *all* Creek land east of the Chattahoochee surveyed for a land lottery, including the areas reserved for the Creek.

President Adams demanded that he stop, and threatened to intervene with federal troops. Troup called Adams' bluff and mobilized the Georgia state militia in response. Fearful of civil war as every president in this era of U.S. history was, Adams eventually backed down and permitted Troup to change the treaty. The governor did so, and swept all of the contested land up for the state.

By 1827, the Creeks were almost completely gone from Georgia, inhabiting only a narrow corridor of land that straddled its modern border with Alabama. Two years later, their old antagonist Andrew Jackson—known to the Creek as "Sharp Knife"—became president.

On March 23, 1829, President Jackson addressed the Creek nation through a letter read by federal Indian Agent Colonel John Crowell. In it, Jackson paid lip service to the traditional religion of the Creek and some other North American tribes by proclaiming that it was "by the permission of the Great Spirit above" that he became president.

Thereafter, Jackson referred to himself as "Father," and to the Creek and other tribes as his "children" or "brothers" whom he loved. From this paternal yet authoritarian position, Jackson's letter described how he would remove the Creek west of the Mississippi for their own good, to protect them from their "white brothers" who would trouble them no longer.

The Treaty of Cusseta

Jackson's grandiose proclamation gave way to three years of tense silence as the Creek declined invitations to discuss Removal and the U.S. government busied itself with the Choctaws, Seminoles, and other groups first. But the settlers encroaching from Georgia and Alabama continued to come, eventually pushing the Creek to their tipping point.

Creek leaders gathered in their village of Kasihta, also known as Cusseta, on March 24, 1832. There they met with U.S. agents who compelled them to accept federal terms and conditions which almost entirely defined the treaty. It was less of a treaty and more of a list of demands, as so many other treaties were in those days.

The Treaty of Cusseta relinquished all Creek claims to ancestral land east of the Mississippi, but did not remove them from it. Instead, it turned tribal land in to private land, and divided it up among those Creek individuals and families who could stay behind. Chiefs could obtain a square mile of land for themselves, while other Creek families could receive up to a half-mile squared. Orphans would also be given land and resources to assimilate to white society as fast as possible.

These land grants were small and would be quickly taken up, justifying the second half of the treaty which the U.S. government cared most about—removing the Creek to land in Indian Territory. The usual offers were made to pay for transportation, as well as one year of life after that. Three hundred and fifty thousand dollars was offered to help them along.

"War"

With all of the tribal land in Georgia gone before this treaty was signed, the Creeks who lived legally on their land were within Alabama borders. Rather than just squatting on Creek land like their neighbors, Alabaman expansionists used more underhanded tactics.

New Creek land owners were mostly inexperienced in a free, European-style land market, or personal ownership of land at all. This was the first plot of land many of them would own as individuals, and they rarely knew the actual value of their property. Land speculators and swindlers started to cheat Creeks out of their land at outrageously low prices.

Once the Creeks wizened up to this over the next four years, they began to resist further encroachment. But state and federal governments routinely ignored the situation or refused to protect their individual rights. The Creek took law in to their own hands then, and started to fight back.

As had been done many times in North American history, a group of Native American warriors lashed out at settlers who had overstepped their boundaries time and again. These small attacks were done as miniature punitive expeditions, meant to correct behavior and reestablish an understanding between the two groups. They were a normal part of Native American warfare and conflict-resolution for centuries.

But Euro-Americans didn't have the context or cultural background to understand that, and so they rarely ever saw those attacks as "only" responses. Instead, the attacks were seen as declarations of war, even if they were done in direct response to recent attacks on Natives. So, when a party of Creek and Yuchi warriors led by Jim Henry burned the small town of Roanoke, Georgia to the ground in the culmination of isolated cases of violence and destruction of property, the federal government mobilized an overwhelming force to crush them.

Stopping cyclical bloodshed was completely legitimate and, in fact, required of any government whose job it is to protect its people, but the way in which the U.S. army approached the Creek "War" of 1826 was not. They saw the isolated attacks by small groups and independent actors as a concerted effort on the part of the entire Creek nation.

Once Jim Henry and his warriors were defeated and captured, the fourteen companies of U.S. army regulars in Alabama proceeded to evict all Creek families from their homes. The conflict had forfeited their treaty rights, according to President Jackson. They would all be Removed to the west.

Creek Trail of Tears

About five thousand Creeks and a few hundred African slaves or their descendants had already been migrated west by 1836, with predictable results and casualties for the Trail of Tears. Now however, the army would force fifteen thousand Creeks to make the trek back-to-back.

The groups of Creek refugees were herded together at Fort Mitchell close to the Chattahoochee River and then marched north and west until they reached Fort Gibson. This was a distance of over seven hundred miles, and because the expulsion period was from the middle of 1836 to the middle of 1837, many of the detachments of Creeks were forced to walk in the winter.

The Creeks did not travel as one enormous group, but were staggered out over time to make logistics easier for the U.S. military. Unfortunately, this meant that by the time the second or third group of Creeks passed through an area, it had been stripped of all-natural resources by those who came before them. Starvation added to mounting deaths by exposure.

Disease epidemics with no facilities or doctors to treat them awaited the Creeks in Indian Territory. Here, they received no help from their army escorts and were promptly abandoned with little more than the clothes on their backs and a single blanket per family. All of their other property was stolen, repossessed, or destroyed.

At least three thousand five hundred Creek men, women, and children died during this last phase of Creek Removal alone. Traditional estimates of total Creek deaths on the Trail of Tears hover at around four thousand. These are mortality rates that would not be seen again on the Trail of Tears for some time. But they would be seen again.

Chapter Seven

Chickasaw Removal

The Chickasaw of Tennessee, Mississippi, and Alabama, allied with the United States at various points in their history as neighbors. This was partly thanks to the robust economy and many "civilizing" qualities the Chickasaw nation adapted over the centuries. And like the Choctaw and Creek, the Chickasaws also had a growing class of cultural ambassadors in the form of mixed-race tribe members who could bridge the gap between Euro-American and Native American society.

One prominent family of mixed Chickasaws was the Colberts. Descended from three high-ranking Chickasaw women who married a Scottish-American man in succession, over a dozen Colbert children would rise to prominent roles in

Chickasaw society at the turn of the nineteenth century thanks to their mothers' status.

The sons of Colbert, in particular, stand out in the historical record as prominent leaders during nearly a century of the Chickasaw's most trying times. The bilingual Colbert boys served as interpreters, negotiators, chiefs, and military allies to the U.S., including Andrew Jackson. Often, Euro-Americans thought them to be "principle chiefs" or otherwise particularly powerful men in the Chickasaw tribe because they did not understand the nation's decentralized government.

This close working relationship may have helped insulate the Chickasaws from the worst of Removal-Era depredations. It did not save them from all of them, however. As with the Creek and Choctaw, having a class of wealthy, landowning chiefs with deep connections to the U.S. government was a double-edged sword.

When land cessions were made, they almost invariably had a Colbert brother or one of their allies involved, and he usually received a private land deed or payment out of the treaty. The Chickasaw lost all of their land in modern Alabama and Tennessee from 1805 to 1818 in this way, despite the fact that they knew how very valuable some of it was.

But the Chickasaw nation as a whole was committed to its own interests and independence, no matter how close to the United States some of its members may have been. When they were the only guests to show up at the failed Franklin Talks of 1830, the Chickasaws drove a hard bargain.

They demanded that before their homeland was taken away, it would be divided up and allotted to individual Chickasaws and families. Then these families would have full control of the sale of their land, and use the profits to buy land in Indian Territory. And, if suitable land could not be found, their obligation toward the agreement would be voided.

As stated earlier, this savvy agreement ultimately fell through with the U.S. government, but that did not take the idea off the table for the Chickasaws. When pressures from the state of Mississippi ramped up over the next two years and federal agents came around to meet for another round of negotiations, the terms returned without an inch given.

Monetary Removal

On October 20, 1832, the Treaty of Pontotoc Creek was signed. Under it, the Chickasaw nation would maintain sovereignty after years of attempts by the state of Mississippi to abolish tribal authority. Chickasaw families would be given individual allotments of their six-million-acre homeland to sell, once sufficient land west of the Mississippi River was found.

Until then, they would be protected from having their land stolen by having it counted as a "temporary homestead." After Supreme Court rulings made it virtually impossible for Native Americans to have title and deed to their land, this was the next best thing to discourage squatters. And instead of having to find land for themselves, the responsibility for finding replacement land for the Chickasaws fell to the U.S. government.

And despite all of the pressure that Mississippi continued to put on them, the Chickasaws only left once they were good and ready to do so. Only in January of 1837, did Chickasaw chiefs sign an agreement stating they approved the land their people would be moving on to.

The five-year span in between was spent shoring up the agreement and managing, with a surprising amount of success, to keep squatters out of unclaimed land until existing Chickasaw homesteads could expand to include it and eventually profit from it.

The source of the new land in Indian Territory was equally surprising. Because of their small numbers compared to other tribes deported from the South, the Chickasaws would be able to fit in to Choctaw land. The Choctaws were faring better than when they had reached their destination back in 1833, and they were in a position to make such an arrangement. Five hundred and thirty thousand dollars saw the westernmost piece of Choctaw land given to the Chickasaws.

With a new homeland guaranteed, the Chickasaws began to sell their property off to Mississippian settlers. Thanks to the large amount of foresight and luck the tribal government had and its people had, the Chickasaws were able to sell their land at much better prices than the Creek had been forced to settle with.

Including what they paid the Choctaws, the Chickasaw tribe made out with three million dollars in land sales. They would not see the vast majority of this money given to them for the next thirty years thanks to obstruction by the U.S. government. But what they did obtain in time, they used to prepare themselves for the journey west.

By this point in time the Trail of Tears, or at least the conditions of it, were becoming well-known. By being latecomers to the tragedy, the Chickasaws could, at least, learn from the misfortune of previously deported tribes. For the first time, a tribe would arrange and pay for its own transportation west.

This was costly, but it guaranteed that the Chickasaws would be furnished for the exodus better than any of the other tribes had been. They would not be forced to rely on government mismanagement or inhumane conditions imposed on them by an impatient U.S. army. To finish their preparations, they would follow the trails that had already been blazed by the Creeks and their new Choctaw neighbors.

Almost miraculously, it worked.

From 1837 to 1838, just under five thousand Chickasaws and over one thousand African slaves made the trek to Indian Territory. Five hundred of them would die along the way. This number was still painful and traumatic for a culture to recover from, but compared to the atrocities faced by other tribes, a loss of less than ten percent almost seems like a lucky break.

As soon as they arrived, the U.S. government began to treat the Chickasaws as part of the Choctaw nation in all of its diplomacy and administration. This dispute would last for decades as both tribes chafed under being lumped together, but fortunately it was resolved without conflict.

It began to seem like Native American Removal was taking a turn toward less destructive, more long-term policies that would respect the basic humanity of those involved. Unfortunately, this trend would not continue.

Chapter Eight

Cherokee Removal

The Cherokee were relatively new arrivals in the American South. Their ancestors were Iroquoian language-speakers who migrated down in to what would become Georgia, where their culture and identity transformed thanks to old Mississippian influences. We do not know why the ancient Cherokee left their northern homeland in the ancient past. But we do know why they left their southern one.

Georgia had always been rich in desirable land and natural resources. For almost as long as they had known one another, settlers wanted the Cherokee off of it. There were legal battles over their land spanning generations, interrupted once in a while by real, bloody battles like Dunmore's War and the Cherokee-American Wars.

When the cotton gin was invented, this land battle intensified. Those Cherokee who *didn't* intensely farm the crop were seen by Euro-Americans as wasting the precious land they subsisted on. Those who *did* grow cotton plantation-style were seen as threats who could compete with white settlers in the market. Therefore, all of them had to go.

But in the late 1820s, a new discovery was made in Georgia that would truly shake the state to its foundations, and literally as well as metaphorically move mountains. Around the county of Dahlonega, Georgia, gold was discovered in the hills.

The Georgia Gold Rush immediately started, attracting thousands of miners, prospectors, and other people who would support the new economy brought with them. It would be a very big boom, followed by a very big bust, and by the 1840s, gold would be extremely difficult to find, leading many to abandon the state and head west to California.

But at the height of the Gold Rush, the Cherokee knew it as the Great Intrusion, because hungry prospectors soon encroached on Cherokee tribal land in search of more of the previous metal. The government took this as incentive to finish the long legal battle and finally Remove the tribe for good.

The legal battle reached the Supreme Court twice in this era, once with the inconclusive *Cherokee Nation v. Georgia*, 1831, and again with much more of an impact in *Worcester v. State of Georgia*. Worcester ruled that Georgia could not impose state laws on Cherokee land, because only the national government had authority over Indian Affairs.

This might have given the Cherokee some breathing room, if not for the reelection of Andrew Jackson in 1832. Indian Removal was as large a part of his platform as ever before, and the federal government proceeded to put pressure on the Cherokee that Georgia could not. The atmosphere became so volatile that in October 1835, John Ross, a mixed-race principle chief of the Cherokee nation, was kidnapped by a Georgian militia.

Fortunately, Ross survived the encounter, and led a delegation to Washington, D.C., to try and lobby against the Removal policy with President Jackson directly. Ross proposed that the Cherokee sell a portion of their land in exchange for money and land west of the Mississippi, which the money could be invested in developing and traveling to. In this, could be seen some of the same wisdom as what the Chickasaws followed.

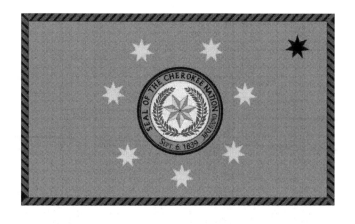

(Source:
https://commons.wikimedia.org/wiki/File:Flag_of_the_Cherokee_Nation.svg)

But Jackson refused this compromise in favor of a complete cession of Cherokee lands at once. John Ross was left haggling with the President over the price that their homeland would go for, but he could not get him to agree to a price. In the end, Ross left with the highly unlikely 'suggestion' of twenty million dollars, to be decided upon by the U.S. Senate.

The Senate ended up agreeing to pay five million dollars, even lower than the modern conservative land value estimate of seven million. This huge power gap between the distant government and the Cherokee actually living on the land caused disputes within the tribe. The majority refused to agree to the terms. But a minority was disaffected and frustrated to the point that they wanted a resolution—any resolution—as quickly as possible.

This was taken advantage of by John F. Schemerhorn, the U.S. Indian Agent assigned to the Cherokee tribe. He gathered this "Treaty Party" of about five hundred Cherokees up at New Echota and drafted a treaty that would cede all Cherokee land to the United States for the Senate's five million dollars, plus five hundred thousand to fund education, as well as compensation for property left behind.

There was also a promising clause which allowed for any Cherokees who wanted to remain in the southeast to become citizens and keep an allotment of about one hundred and sixty acres per family for themselves. That clause tipped the vote toward unanimity, though it would later be removed by President Jackson, forcing all Cherokees to walk the Trail of Tears.

It would force them along the Trail of Tears because, despite how the majority of Cherokees and their national council decried this 1835 Treaty of New Echota as illegitimate, Congress ratified it by one vote and treated it as legally binding. John Ross and other chiefs fought for a repeal, with no success. If the Cherokee were seen as going back on their word now, they would have to answer to the military.

Waves of Removal

The treaty was implemented as soon as it was ratified, beginning a two-year grace period during which the Cherokee were expected to prepare for their own Removal. Removal of the Cherokee occurred in waves, as the case had been with almost every other tribe on the Trail of Tears.

The first waves were of voluntary Removal, mostly by the Cherokee families who had been part of or supported the Treaty Party. The voluntary period is synonymous with the treaty's grace period from 1835 to 1837. While Chief Ross and his followers urged the Cherokee people to refuse the provisions offered by U.S. army officials who began entering Cherokee land, pro-Removal groups urged the opposite.

The pro-Removal group believed that the essence of the Cherokee nation was its people, rather than its land, and saw the fight to cling to their home in the east as futile and harmful. They believed with some truth that racism and opportunism were too deep in Euro-American society for Native American rights to ever be truly respected. They believed that safety would come from flight, if only temporarily.

When the grace period ended in 1838, almost all of the pro-Removal camp had left Cherokee land. They were fewer than two thousand, and made up a very small part of the Cherokee nation. But keeping with the trend of lighter population transfers causing fewer fatalities, the Removal camp was able to migrate west under historically lackluster army oversight with less than one hundred deaths.

This group joined with the so-called "Old Settler" Cherokee, who had migrated west in previous decades. Together they numbered maybe six thousand. They left behind over fourteen thousand "National Party" Cherokee, who were still led in passive resistance by principle chief John Ross and the Cherokee National Council.

The deadline for voluntary Removal passed on May 23, 1838. After this point, the U.S. government began to mobilize military force to threaten the resistant Cherokee with. By this stage the atrocities of the Trail of Tears were growing well-known even among distant white Americans, and the opposition to Indian Removal was as strong as ever.

But Andrew Jackson's successor as president, Martin van Buren, followed in his footsteps with regards to Native American policy after being elected in 1837. No protests or strongly-worded letters would dissuade him from the course things had been set upon.

Van Buren authorized General William Scott to oversee the deportation of all remaining Cherokee. Arriving in New Echota in May with over seven thousand soldiers and state militia at his command, he set about rounding them up.

Somewhat surprisingly, General Scott was adamant in showing the Cherokees respect and kindness. He ordered his troops to do the same, and even threatened to arrest soldiers who abused their wards. Unfortunately, not even a U.S. general had any real power to protect Native Americans from the volatile situation that had been made.

By June 2nd, scattered Cherokee communities across Alabama, Tennessee, and North Carolina, were being herded in to concentration camps at gunpoint, their homes and most of their possessions abandoned. About one thousand Cherokees fled in to the mountains to escape the roundup, but thousands more were caught.

After they were driven together like cattle, the Cherokee were made to march to the Tennessee River, where they would wait at ports in modern day Chattanooga and Guntersville for steamers and flatboats to ferry them across the river. A drought struck and dropped the water level low enough to mire the boats in mud and other obstacles, requiring their passengers to disembark and walk at points.

This Tennessee River fiasco, alongside the violence of the roundup and the conditions of the clustered camps, killed at least two hundred Cherokee. It was a bad enough blunder for General Scott to order a halt to all Removal efforts in early September. Eleven internment camps were built for the Cherokee to wait in until Removal could resume.

Many of the deaths on the Trail of Tears occurred during harsh, wet winters. But here, languishing in the unseasonably dry 1838 summer, the Cherokee faced the equally terrible flip-side of that coin. Breakouts of dysentery and other infectious diseases thriving in overcrowded, hot places hit the Cherokee hard, killing over three hundred and fifty more as they waited like prisoners behind wooden palisades.

Eventually, something had to give. Army coordination wasn't getting better any time soon, and with so many of his people dying, principle chief John Ross finally gave up hope of avoiding Removal. He negotiated to personally oversee it, and to have responsibility transferred from the U.S. Army to the Cherokee themselves, similar to how the Chickasaws had handled their own migration.

To his credit, General Scott agreed to this plan despite how expensive it would be, and how many people it angered in the U.S. government. Andrew Jackson was absolutely livid, but there was nothing Old Hickory could do about it as a former president.

With expenses paid by the army, Ross and his people got right to work. The Cherokee National Council conferred on him temporary but greater power within the tribe, making him, for the first time, what the U.S. always assumed a principle chief to be.

Using this power, Ross organized the surviving Cherokee in to twelve wagon trains and delegated roles and responsibilities to each train's leaders. He ensured that every train had physicians, English-Cherokee interpreters, teamsters, quartermasters, gravediggers, and anyone else that they expected to need on the harsh two thousand two-hundred-mile march. They even pooled the money to buy the steamboat *Victoria* so that Ross and other chiefs could traverse rivers quickly—and in relative comfort.

This was the reluctant Removal, and despite all the preparations made it would be the deadliest wave. The summer delay was appreciated at first, but soon the tolerable cool turned to bitter cold as winter settled in and Cherokee trains took more northerly trails toward Indian Territory. Snowstorms blew in, followed by an epidemic of pneumonia.

The exact number of Cherokee who died on the Trail of Tears is uncertain, but doctors who traveled with their wagon trains made the educated guess of about four thousand men, women, and children. This number is supported by census results from before and after Removal.

In the fall of 1835, a census of the Cherokee nation in the east counted over eighteen thousand people, made up of about sixteen thousand ethnic Cherokees and a minority of African slaves and intermarried Euro-Americans. In the end of 1838, only twelve thousand Cherokee appear on the Indian Territory census. Still, as many as six to eight thousand could have died in the immediate aftermath of the Removal.

The Cherokee migration is what many people think of first when they hear the phrase "Trail of Tears," and for good reason. It was one of the biggest, most protracted Indian Removals of the era, and among its deadliest and most tragic.

But it was still just one of many forced population transfers which had been occurring for centuries before, and which would happen again for almost another century.

Chapter Nine

Other Tribe Removals

The small stories deserve attention as much as the large ones, and though the Five Tribes were affected most famously by the Trail of Tears, others suffered and survived its trials as well. Ponca, Ojibwa, Ho-Chunk, Sauk, Fox, Iowa, Illinois, and Potawatomi, and many other tribes as far north as the Great Lakes and the Dakotas were driven from their lands during and after the height of southeastern Indian Removal.

The Ponca tribe is a small but historically significant Siouan language-speaking tribe. They may have migrated west across the Mississippi alongside other Siouan people in the pre-colonial era to escape Iroquois expansion in the east. By the time they were signing their first treaties with the

United States in 1817, they were located in modern-day Nebraska.

Between 1817 and 1865, the Ponca signed a series of treaties with the U.S. government that ceded more and more of their land in order to take the pressure of speculators and squatters off of them. It was also done as part of an effort to reduce conflict with their larger, more powerful neighbors.

The U.S. was not bent on complete control of the Old Northwest at this point in time, but they still wanted stable borders and buffer states. The Ponca was convenient in this regard. The tribe was small and mobile, and more easily able to pick up and move, or to be forced to.

Unfortunately for the Ponca, they were such a small tribe that they eventually went unnoticed in the signing of one of these Northwestern treaties. In the 1868 Treaty of Fort Laramie with the Sioux, the U.S. forgot that the Ponca had been resettled in an area that the government was now ceding to the Sioux as part of their new reservation in Nebraska and South Dakota.

Within a few years, the situation between the Ponca and Sioux tribes moving in to their land grew hostile. Both sides believed the land to be rightfully theirs. In the end, the U.S.

government arbitrated the situation and made the cold, pragmatic decision to evict the much smaller and weaker Ponca tribe.

By 1876, the tribe was being driven south to Indian Territory to land which their chiefs had surveyed and reportedly hated. Less than ten people died during the initial march, but in a tribe of less than seven hundred people, their loss—including the daughters of head Chief Standing Bear—was felt just as dearly.

(Source: https://commons.wikimedia.org/wiki/File:Standingbear.jpg)

After more than two grueling years of starvation, malaria, and the hot Oklahoman climate that they were not used to, up to a third of the Ponca died. This included one of Standing Bear's last remaining children, Bear Shield. The situation seemed untenable.

In response, several dozen Ponca led by Chief Standing Bear ignored the laws keeping them on the reservation and went north again. Many of the Ponca brought the dead with them. Standing Bear carried the body of his son, whom he swore to bury in the tribe's ancestral homelands back in Nebraska.

This band of Ponca made it to the Omaha Reservation before they were captured, and Standing Bear was imprisoned by the U.S. army. His story gained notoriety, yet he was held until his habeas corpus suit reached the district court. In *Omaha v. Crook*, 1879, it was ruled for the first time in American history that Native Americans are "persons" within the meaning of the law.

That is to say, for the first time in over a century of the United States' existence, the equal humanity of a Native American under its law was confirmed. For the first time, Native entitlement to civil rights and protection were explicitly acknowledged. Everything before this was merely a suggestion, and an oft-ignored one at that.

It came after centuries of undue treatment, but it was a landslide case in Native American civil rights. The dichotomy of Native tribes being subjects yet aliens would finally be chipped away at. Not quite two decades after Africans had finally thrown off the yoke of slavery and asserted their humanity, Natives were able to do the same in part.

Standing Bear was freed and allowed to mourn his son. The Ponca he brought with him were able to repurchase some of their old land and settle it, which is why today there are two recognized Ponca tribes in Oklahoma and Nebraska.

The Ponca aren't unique in being split up by their personal Trail of Tears experiences. The Ho-Chunk/Winnebago people of the Great Lakes region were steadily pushed west by rival tribes and European expansion over the centuries, and with each forced migration the tribe grew fragmented. Eventually they made something of a homeland in modern Wisconsin, but that would be temporary as well.

Starting in 1836, the Ho-Chunk faced a staggering thirteen Removals in a row as they were pushed through Minnesota, the Dakotas, and Nebraska. In 1846, there was an estimated four thousand four hundred Ho-Chunk, but by 1848, relocation and smallpox cut them almost by half to two thousand five hundred.

Every step along the way they did all they could to resist and keep their homes, but this only fragmented them worse. In the end, the remains of the tribe were split by hundreds of miles, and today make up the separate tribes of the Ho-Chunk of Wisconsin and the Winnebago of Nebraska, respectively.

Dozens of other small bands and tribes from the Old Northwest suffered a similar fate as they were moved around like so many puzzle pieces by the game-masters of the U.S. government. Many did not go without some form of resistance like their southern neighbors. The Sauk, Fox, and Kickapoo tribes did not move until the military defeat of their legendary leader, Black Hawk.

While their losses might seem negligible individually, the northwestern tribes add up to be as much as a fourth of the total deaths on the Trail of Tears.

Chapter Ten

Consequences

It is difficult to put in to words the level of destruction that the Trail of Tears caused. Deaths, political corruption, and statistics can be agonized over, but the human anguish and the loss of culture are incalculable. Even after surviving their first years on their new reservations, Native Americans rarely saw an end to their hardships.

The most immediate challenge faced by all tribes, but especially the Five Civilized Tribes, was building a new home large and stable enough to house their surviving populations. Towns had to be erected from scratch if none of their people had migrated to Indian Territory previously. Schools and other specialized buildings needed to be staffed by experts who were often Euro-Americans on temporary loan from the government.

Industries transformed or ceased altogether. People formerly employed as hunters and trappers in the lucrative fur and skin trades of their forested homes now had to turn to farming. Longtime agriculturalists no longer had the land or the crops they had known so well. Slave-owning plantation farmers generally had the resources to reestablish themselves comfortably, but the common people often faced a life of limited subsistence.

Some Natives benefited from the conditions which surrounded their eventual Removal, but cases like that were far and few between. Most prominently, Cherokees who had learned about prospecting from the Georgia Gold Rush were later able to do their own prospecting in the later gold rushes of California and other parts of the west.

There was political and social upheaval as well as economic. Tribes, which had once been very decentralized, took steps toward more structured, hierarchical government as a form of protection.

Principle chief, once a Euro-American designation, turned in to an elected position held within semi-republican governments with their own constitutions and specialized branches. Native Americans had always established and lived in nations, but they now resembled modern states too.

This political centralization responded to some of the irreparable splits formed in each tribe by Removal. None of the tribes migrated west were moved with one hundred percent effectiveness. Whether by owning private property, or making other settlements with state governments, or by simply fleeing to a remote corner of the country and escaping notice, many pockets of Native Americans avoided the Trail of Tears.

They rarely numbered more than a few dozen or hundreds, but these isolated groups survived and carried on their culture as best as they could. Like the Ponca and Ho-Chunk split across the Midwest, the Five Tribes left splinter tribes in the Southeast.

For example, the Cherokee of Oklahoma call themselves the Cherokee Nation today, but there is also recognition for the Eastern Band of Cherokee Indians in North Carolina, and the United Keetoowah Band of Cherokee Indians descended from the Old Settlers of Arkansas. The Muscogee—Creek—Nation is headquartered in Oklahoma, yet their descended Coushatta tribes exist in Louisiana and Texas. And to this day, the Seminoles of Florida have not given up their swamps.

The Indian Territory nations remained the largest and strongest despite the damage they'd faced in migrating, and for much of the latter half of the nineteenth century they would be major players in North American politics. This also meant that the final pieces of the stage were set for the Civil War which the U.S. had been creeping toward for decades.

Native Americans in the American Civil War

When the inevitable conflict between federal power and state autonomy broke out in the United States, Native American tribes participated in the Civil War. Just like when they would play one European power against the other in the colonial days, the tribes sided with the Union or the Confederacy as a way to make a powerful ally or hinder a more powerful enemy.

Most tribes across the whole of the U.S. sided with the Union, but members of the Five Tribes—as well as the Catawba—allied with or had sympathies for the Confederacy at some point. A few years of separation and a common enemy turned the tribes and the states that had pushed them out in to unlikely friends.

The lower centralization and the greater perceived respect for sovereign Native American nations by the Confederates also endeared many Indian Territory chiefs and bands who wanted to keep their independence. Tribes with growing slave-based economies like the Choctaw and Chickasaw also shared the major issue of pro-slavery in common with the Confederacy.

Even as allies, tribes were hesitant to over-commit. They rarely sent battalions of soldiers beyond their own borders to fight, and they defaulted to neutrality when a Union victory in their theater of the war was certain.

The Cherokee only sided with the South after they were torn apart by their own civil war, and Principle Chief John Ross' neutral camp was defeated by the growing pro-Confederate movement led by one Stand Watie.

Stand Watie rose to the rank of General in the Confederate army, the only Native American to attain such a rank, and he was the last Confederate commander to surrender in the entire war. He even outlasted Robert E. Lee by two months.

Looking Ahead

The devastation of the war came less than two decades after the tribes had been forced west, dragging out the process of state-building back home. Another two decades would see the United States eating away at reservation land through legislation, like the 1887 Dawes Act, which converted all tribal land to private property and then sold "surplus" land off to non-natives.

This was another blatant land-grab which went against the letter and the spirit of the agreements which sent Native Americans west to begin with. The sovereignty and freedom promised by isolation was undermined as soon as the governments of neighboring states and territories found it convenient to do so.

By this point, it was the turn of the twentieth century. This means that the modern day social and political condition of Native Americans, as well as the United States relationship to them, were created as a direct result of the Indian Removal Act.

The splits in tribes caused by incomplete Removal were only social and cultural at first. But they became highly political when tribes started to require official federal recognition from the U.S., and benefits from tribe membership began to be defined by a certain level of blood descent.

Suddenly the descendants of freedmen in the Cherokee, Seminole, and other tribes would find themselves written in or out of the narratives of their own societies, depending on how many resources there were to share. New hierarchies formed within communities, created by outside causes.

Eventually a complicated, uneven dynamic was settled on. Tribal nations would continue to exist to some degree as a social and political group, with rights and limited internal autonomy guaranteed by newer legislation like the Indian Reorganization Act of 1934.

Tribal law generally survived, but it had to fit in and around federal and state or local law in a way befitting "domestic dependent nations." Where one jurisdiction ended and another began was not—and still isn't—always clear. At times, these disputes are over land use. The more things change, the more they stay the same.

Attempts would be made after this point to abolish tribes and push for assimilation, but Native American political organization as well as public opinion of the country at large would generally protect the new *status quo*. The Five Tribes and others survived the Trail of Tears, and they will survive for the foreseeable future.

Cultural Impact

While some details of the event are rarely taught and even more rarely remembered, the Trail of Tears is one of the most infamous pieces of American history. Countless books, performances, paintings, songs, films, and other forms of cultural reference to the Removal can be found throughout modern America.

Some of them are based on fact, while others are fictional and take inspiration and historical context from the Removals. All of them share in common a desire by their creators to understand and contextualize what happened, and what it means to American and Native American identities today.

The United States government has also participated in this practice of cultural remembrance. Despite—or perhaps because of—its involvement in the Trail of Tears, departments of state and federal governments have been establishing and maintaining landmarks, monuments, memorials, and educational centers like museums dedicated to the Trail of Tears for decades.

One can even travel along the preserved trails that the deported tribes walked generations ago. Thousands of miles of wilderness trails and water routes have been authorized as an official Trail of Tears National Historic trail. It crosses the borders of nine states and charts the courses of many of the tribes removed from the Southeast, especially the Cherokee with whom the Trail of Tears has become almost synonymous.

These trails are often visited and walked by tourists, as well as the descendants of those who made the first march down them. Through ritual remembrance of past traumas, Native tribes are able to heal old wounds. It also allows them to turn something that was once a destroyer of their cultures in to a powerful and positive source of solidarity and identity.

Conclusion

The Trail of Tears was a forced migration of unprecedented size and speed in American history. It caused the deaths of tens of thousands of people and disrupted hundreds of years of tradition across dozens of cultures. It was the simultaneous manipulation of people as if they were subjects, and the "othering" of them as though they were aliens.

It fundamentally transformed the political and social landscape of North America, and paved the way for the United States to expand from coast to coast, along with everything that implies. It was a jarring change, as well as an inhumane logistical blunder, yet we wouldn't be able to recognize our world today without it.

The Trail of Tears was not a shockingly sudden, isolated event in history, however. It was a culmination of many causes and many earlier atrocities—land disputes, culture clash, failed or broken diplomacy, racism, etc. And it was not a conclusion of any of those things. The descendants of the people who were forced to walk those trails are still struggling with the repercussions. The U.S. still struggles with its legacy.

But it offers Native Americans and the United States both a valuable lesson. It demonstrates the adaptability, resourcefulness, and indomitable spirit of people who were, for centuries, considered uncivilized and savage. It shows governments what shortsighted, greedy things not to do when relating to the indigenous people of their lands.

Ultimately, the story draws attention to the cruelty that we can inflict upon one another despite the shared humanity of all people. It asks a reflecting observer why something like this happened, and tasks them to never let something like it happen again.

References

Byrd, Billie. "The Migration To The West Of The Muskogees." University of Oklahoma Libraries. 1937. http://digital.libraries.ou.edu/cdm/ref/collection/indianpp/id/1513

Lawler, Andrew. *The Secret Token: Myth, Obsession, and the Search for the Lost Colony of Roanoke*. New York: Doubleday. 2018.

Zacek, Natalie. "Bartholomew Gosnold (1571–August 22, 1607)." *Encyclopedia Virginia*. Virginia Foundation for the Humanities, 21 May 2014. https://www.encyclopediavirginia.org/Gosnold_Bartholomew_1571-August_22_1607#start_entry

Sultzman, Lee. "Wampanoag History." Tolatsga.org. Retrieved 30 November 2008. http://www.tolatsga.org/wampa.html

Fausz, J. Frederick. "The 'Barbarous Massacre' Reconsidered: The Powhatan Uprising of 1622 and the Historians." *Explorations in Ethnic Studies*. 1978.

Trigger, Bruce G. Washburn, Wilcomb E. *The Cambridge History of the Native Peoples of the Americas*

Volume 1, North America, Part 1. Cambridge University Press. 1996.

Adam King (2002). "Mississippian Period: Overview." New Georgia Encyclopedia. Retrieved 15 Nov 2009. https://www.georgiaencyclopedia.org/articles/history-archaeology/mississippian-period-overview

Groneman, William. *David Crockett: Hero of the Common Man*. New York. Forge Books. 2005.

Foreman, Grant. *Indian Removal*. The University of Oklahoma Press. 1953.

Sandra Faiman-Silva. *Choctaws at the Crossroads*. University of Nebraska Press. 1997.

DeRosier, Arthur H. *The Removal of the Choctaw Indians*. The University of Tennessee Press Knoxville. 1970.

Missall, John and Mary Lou Missal. *Seminole Wars: America's Longest Indian Conflict*. University Press of Florida. 2004.

Favorite, Merab-Michal. *Bradenton*. Arcadia Publishing. 2013.

Gray & Bowen. *The American Annual Register for the Year 1829-30*. G & C Carvill. 1832.

Maloney, Christopher. "Treaty of Cusseta (1832)." Encyclopedia of Alabama. 2011. http://www.encyclopediaofalabama.org/article/h-3083

Kane, Robert B. "Second Creek War." Encyclopedia of Alabama. 2016. http://www.encyclopediaofalabama.org/article/h-3866

Anderson, William L. *Cherokee Removal: Before and After*. The University of Georgia Press. 1991.

"The Ponca Trail of Tears." Nebraska Studies. http://nebraskastudies.org/1875-1899/the-trial-of-standing-bear/the-ponca-trail-of-tears/

Pauls, Elizabeth Prine. "Trail of Tears." Encyclopedia Britannica. https://www.britannica.com/event/Trail-of-Tears

National Park Service. "Trail of Tears." NPS. https://www.nps.gov/trte/index.htm

About History Compacted

Here in History Compacted, we see history as a large collection of stories. Each of these amazing stories of the past can help spark ideas for the future. However, history is often proceeded as boring and incomprehensible. That is why it is our mission to simplify the fascinating stories of history.

Follow History Compacted:

Website: www.historycompacted.com

Twitter: @HistoryCompact

Facebook: https://www.facebook.com/historycompacted/

Instagram: @history_compacted

Dark Minds In History

For updates about new releases, as well as exclusive promotions, sign up for our newsletter and you can also receive a free book today. Thank you and see you soon.

Sign up here: http://bit.ly/2ToHti3

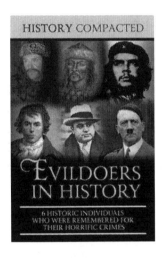

Evildoers in History: 6 Historic Individuals Remembered For Their Horrific Crimes is a book that explores the stories of six infamous criminals in history, these evildoers were not remembered by their countless murders but by the brutality with which they took the lives of their victims. There is no other term to describe them but ruthless, as you will soon find out.

Prepare yourself, the gruesome part of history is not for everyone...

Made in the USA
San Bernardino, CA
27 January 2020